Planting Change

Embracinng Veganism Through the Power of Plants

Payam Mohseni

ISBN: 979-8-218-97239-4

Table of Contents

Introduction

n a world brimming with choices, there exists a remarkable force, often overlooked and underestimated: the
power of plants. These living beings, rooted in the earth,
can profoundly shape our lives, nourish our bodies, and
transform our perspectives. Beyond their role as a source
of sustenance and beauty, plants have become a catalyst
for change—a means to embrace a sustainable and compassionate lifestyle. In "Planting Change: Embracing Veganism through the Power of Plants," we embark on a transformative journey that explores the vast potential of plants
and their pivotal role in revolutionizing our health, planet,
and ethical choices.

Within the enchanting tapestry of the natural world,
plants stand as unparalleled guardians of our well-being.
This book unfolds the vibrant canvas that is the power of
plants, illuminating their extraordinary capabilities and

the profound impact they have on our lives. As we venture deeper, we discover the advantages of a plant-based diet. This path can lead to enhanced vitality, optimal health, and a profound sense of interconnectedness with the natural world.

Through scientific research and experience, we delve into the essential nutrients and healing properties of plants. We unravel the intricate dance between our bodies and the plant kingdom, exploring how these remarkable organisms provide us with the sustenance we need to thrive. Moreover, we delve into the environmental implications of our dietary choices, unraveling the urgent need to embrace sustainable practices and reduce our ecological footprint.

Beyond the physical realm, this book also discusses the ethical dimensions of embracing veganism more than just a diet. This lifestyle extends compassion and empathy to all sentient beings. We confront common misconceptions and dispel prevailing myths, empowering readers with knowledge and understanding. By dismantling barriers and inviting open dialogue, I hope to pave the way for an inclusive exploration of veganism that celebrates diversity and nurtures learning.

"Planting Change: Embracing Veganism through the Power of Plants" is not just a book; it is a call to action, an invitation if you like to embark on a transformative journey towards a sustainable, compassionate future. As the seeds of change take root within our hearts and minds, we unlock the immense potential within the power of plants. Together, we cultivate a world where our choices resonate with harmony within ourselves and the delicate ecosystems that sustain us.

Whether your curiosity stems from an ethical, environmental, or health standpoint, hopefully this book can be your guiding light. This book welcomes all, whether you seek to deepen your understanding of veganism and plant-based diets or simply embark on a journey of vegan-curious exploration. Within these pages, you will find the knowledge, insights, and inspiration to embrace a lifestyle that harmonizes compassion, sustainability, and optimal well-being.

CHAPTER 1

Power of Plants

Plants are more than just a source of food and decoration; they possess a remarkable power beyond their physical presence. From providing essential nutrients to promoting environmental sustainability, plants profoundly impact our health, the planet, and even our ethical choices. In recent years, there has been a growing interest in plant-based diets and the benefits they offer.

This book delves into the power of plants, exploring the advantages of a plant-based diet, the components of a vegan lifestyle, and debunking common myths and misconceptions about veganism.

Understanding the benefits of a plant-based / healthy vegan diet:

A plant-based diet is centered around consuming foods derived from plants, such as fruits, vegetables, whole grains, legumes, nuts, and seeds while minimizing or eliminating the consumption of animal products. Numerous studies have demonstrated the health benefits associated with plant-based eating patterns. Occasionally people assume that a Vegan diet is automatically a healthy diet, which is only sometimes the case.

One of the wonderful things about a plant-based diet is its positive impact on your heart's health. Plant-based diets are typically low in saturated fats and cholesterol, commonly found in animal products. By avoiding or reducing the intake of these harmful components and over-processed food (vegan-friendly or not), individuals following a plant-based diet can lower their risk of developing cardiovascular diseases, including heart attacks and strokes.

Moreover, plant-based diets are rich in fiber, crucial in maintaining a healthy digestive system. Fiber aids digestion, helps prevent constipation, and promotes the growth of beneficial gut bacteria. Additionally, a high-fiber diet has been linked to a reduced risk of chronic conditions, such as type 2 diabetes, obesity, and certain types of cancer.

Another significant benefit of a plant-based diet is its potential for weight management. Plant-based foods are nutrient-dense and lower in calories than animal products. By prioritizing whole, unprocessed plant foods, individuals can feel satisfied while consuming fewer calories, making it easier to maintain a healthy weight or achieve weight loss goals.

Exploring the nutritional components of a vegan lifestyle:

Contrary to common misconceptions, a well-planned plant-based diet can provide all the nutrients for optimal health. While some nutrients are more abundant in animal products, they can be obtained through plant-based alternatives or appropriate supplementation.

Protein is a crucial nutrient often associated with meat and dairy products. However, plant-based protein sources, such as legumes, tofu, tempeh, seitan, and quinoa, can adequately fulfill the body's protein requirements. By combining different plant protein sources throughout the day, individuals can ensure they receive all the essential amino acids.

Omega-3 fatty acids are vital for brain health and reducing inflammation. While fish is commonly known as a rich source of omega-3s, plant-based options like flaxseeds, chia seeds, hemp seeds, and walnuts provide an alternative source of these essential fatty acids. Incorporating these foods into a plant-based diet can help maintain a balanced omega-3 to omega-6 ratio.

Vitamin B12, primarily found in animal products, is often a concern for vegans. However, fortified plant-based foods, such as plant milks, cereals, and nutritional yeast, as well as B12 supplements, can quickly meet the recommended intake of this vital nutrient. It's essential for individuals following a vegan lifestyle to be mindful of their B12 intake and ensure they are meeting their nutritional needs.

Debunking common myths and misconceptions about veganism:

Veganism has been subject to various myths and misconceptions that can deter individuals from adopting a plant-based lifestyle. By debunking these misunderstandings, we can better understand veganism's potential benefits.

One common myth is that a plant-based diet lacks sufficient protein. As mentioned earlier, plants offer a wide range of protein sources that meet the body's protein requirements when consumed in adequate amounts and combinations. A vegan diet can provide all the essential amino acids for overall health and muscle function.

Another misconception is that vegans are at a higher risk of nutrient deficiencies. While it is essential to be mindful of certain nutrients, such as vitamin B12 and omega-3 fatty acids, a balanced and varied plant-based diet can provide all the necessary nutrients for good health. Vegans can maintain optimal nutrition by considering food choices and potentially supplementing specific nutrients.

There is also a belief that veganism is expensive. While certain vegan specialty products can be pricier, a plant-based diet can be more affordable than a meat-centric one. Staples such as fruits, vegetables, grains, legumes, and nuts are often budget-friendly and can be purchased in bulk. Individuals can adopt a cost-effective vegan lifestyle by focusing on whole, unprocessed plant foods.

Lastly, some argue that veganism is restrictive and lacks taste and variety. However, the range of available plant-based options is vast and continuously expanding. From colorful fruits and vegetables to diverse grains, legumes, and plant-based alternatives for meat and dairy, there are countless delicious and satisfying options for vegans. With creativity and exploration, a plant-based diet can be a flavorful and exciting culinary experience.

In conclusion, the power of plants goes beyond their nutritional value. Embracing a plant-based diet can benefit our health, the environment, and animal welfare. By understanding the advantages of a plant-based diet, exploring the nutritional components of a vegan lifestyle, and debunking common myths and misconceptions about veganism, individuals can make informed choices that align with their values and contribute to a healthier and more sustainable future.

CHAPTER 2

Essential Nutrients for Vegans: Ensuring a Balanced Plant-Based Diet

A vegan diet excludes all animal products and can provide excellent nutrition when adequately planned. Vegans must also ensure they meet their nutritional needs by including various plant-based sources. As mentioned in the previous chapter, there is a misconception that if someone is Vegan, they are automatically healthy, which is not necessarily true. We will discuss essential nutrients for vegans or someone following a plant-based diet, including protein, iron, calcium, and omega-3 fatty acids. Practical tips on combining foods for optimal nutrient absorption will also be provided.

Protein: Protein is an essential nutrient for cell repair, growth, and maintenance. While animal products are high in protein, vegans can obtain ample amounts through plant-based sources such as legumes (beans, lentils, chickpeas), soy products (tofu, tempeh), quinoa, seitan, nuts, and seeds. Consuming various sources throughout the day is essential to ensure adequate protein intake. Combining grains and legumes (e.g., rice and beans) form a complete protein, providing all essential amino acids the body requires. Protein-rich snacks like hummus with whole-grain pita or nut butter with whole-grain bread can also contribute to meeting protein needs.

Iron: Iron plays a crucial role in oxygen transport and is particularly important for vegans as plant-based iron is less readily absorbed than iron from animal sources. However, with careful planning, vegans can meet their iron requirements. Good plant-based sources of iron include dark leafy greens (spinach, kale), legumes, fortified cereals, whole grains, tofu, and seeds (pumpkin, sesame). Iron absorption can be enhanced by consuming vitamin C and iron-rich foods. For example, enjoying a citrus fruit salad with spinach or squeezing lemon juice over lentil soup can boost iron absorption. Cooking with cast-iron cookware can also increase the iron content in food.

Calcium: Calcium is vital for strong bones and teeth, nerve function, and muscle contraction. Although dairy products are a common source of calcium, vegans can obtain adequate amounts from plant-based sources. Fortified plant milks (soy, almond, rice), calcium-set tofu, fortified orange juice, dark leafy greens (collard greens, bok choy), almonds, and sesame seeds are excellent sources of calcium. Consuming foods rich in vitamin D, such as fortified plant milks or spending time in sunlight, helps the body absorb and utilize calcium effectively. Including calcium-rich foods in meals and snacks, like a kale and almond salad or a calcium-fortified smoothie, ensures an adequate intake.

Omega-3: Omega-3 fatty acids are essential for brain health, heart function, and reducing inflammation. While fish and seafood are traditional sources of omega-3s, vegans can obtain them from plant-based sources. The primary plant-based omega-3 fatty acid is alpha-linolenic acid (ALA), found in flaxseeds, chia seeds, hemp seeds, walnuts, and their oils. To maximize omega-3 absorption, grinding flaxseeds and consuming them shortly after grinding is beneficial. Additionally, including seaweed and algae-derived omega-3 supplements can provide essential EPA and DHA fatty acids typically found in fish. These supplements are derived from marine algae and are suitable for vegans.

Practical Tips for Optimal Nutrient Absorption

- Combine vitamin C-rich foods with iron-rich foods to enhance iron absorption.

- Soak legumes and grains before cooking to improve nutrient availability and digestion.

- Consume various whole grains, including quinoa, brown rice, and whole wheat products, for nutrient diversity.

- Sprouting seeds, beans, and grains can increase their nutrient content and digestibility.

- Include fermented foods like tempeh, miso, sauerkraut, and kimchi to support gut health and nutrient absorption.

- Use iodized salt or sea vegetables like nori, kombu, or dulse to meet iodine requirements, which are essential for thyroid function.

- Plan meals to incorporate a wide range of colorful fruits and vegetables, ensuring a diverse intake of vitamins, minerals, and antioxidants.

- Consider fortified foods, such as plant milk, cereals, and nutritional yeast, to ensure adequate intake of essential nutrients like B12, vitamin D, and calcium.

- Consult a registered dietitian or nutritionist specializing in vegan nutrition to ensure personalized dietary advice and address specific needs.

A well-planned plant-based diet can provide all essential nutrients, ensuring optimal health. Vegans can maintain a balanced and nourishing plant-based diet by focusing on protein, iron, calcium, and omega-3 fatty acids and implementing practical tips for nutrient absorption. Remember to prioritize variety, enjoy a colorful plate, and seek professional guidance when needed to support your nutritional goals on a vegan lifestyle journey.

CHAPTER 3:

Vegan Pantry Staples

Building a well-stocked pantry is essential for any home cook, which also holds true for vegans. Stocking your kitchen with crucial vegan ingredients gives you the foundation to create delicious and nutritious plant-based meals.

Plant-Based Alternatives to Animal Products

a. **Non-Dairy Milks:** Replace cow's milk with a variety of non-dairy alternatives such as almond milk, soy milk, oat milk, or coconut milk. These plant-based milks can be used in cooking, baking, or enjoyed independently.

b. **Plant-Based Protein Sources:** Incorporate plant-based protein options like tofu, tempeh, seitan, and legumes (beans, lentils, chickpeas) into your pantry. These versatile ingredients can create hearty main dishes, stir-fries, and protein-packed salads.

c. **Vegan Butter and Margarine:** Substitute traditional butter with vegan butter or margarine made from plant oils. They can be used in baking, spreading on bread, or for sautéing and cooking.

d. **Egg Replacers:** Replace eggs in baking with ingredients like applesauce, mashed bananas, flaxseed meal, or chia seeds mixed with water. These alternatives bind ingredients together and provide moisture, just like eggs.

e. **Vegan Cheese:** Explore the wide variety of vegan cheeses available, made from plant-based ingredients like nuts, soy, or tapioca starch. These cheeses can be used in sandwiches, pasta dishes, or enjoyed as a snack.

Essential Pantry Staples

a. **Whole Grains:** Stock your pantry with a variety of whole grains like quinoa, brown rice, oats, barley, and whole wheat pasta. These provide fiber and essential nutrients and serve as a base for many vegan dishes.

b. **Nuts and Seeds:** Include a selection of nuts such as almonds, walnuts, cashews and seeds like flaxseeds, chia seeds, and sunflower seeds. They add texture and flavor and provide healthy fats and protein to your meals and snacks.

c. **Legumes and Pulses:** Keep a variety of canned and dried legumes such as beans, lentils, and chickpeas. These are excellent protein, fiber, and essential minerals sources and can be used in soups, stews, curries, and salads.

d. **Herbs and Spices:** Build a collection of herbs and spices to enhance the flavor of your vegan dishes. Basics like basil, oregano, paprika, cumin, turmeric, and garlic powder can add depth and complexity to your meals.

e. **Nutritional Yeast:** This deactivated yeast is a popular ingredient among vegans due to its cheesy flavor.

It can be used as a topping for popcorn, added to sauces and dressings, or incorporated into vegan "cheese" recipes.

f. **Condiments and Sauces:** Stock up on staples like soy sauce, tamari, tahini, mustard, maple syrup, and vegan mayonnaise. These condiments and sauces can add richness and depth to your dishes.

g. **Vegetable Broth and Bouillon:** Having vegetable broth or bouillon cubes on hand allows you to create flavorful soups, stews, and sauces without needing meat-based stocks.

h. **Canned Tomatoes and Tomato Paste:** These pantry staples form the base of many sauces, stews, and soups. They are versatile and provide depth and acidity to various dishes.

Unique and Versatile Ingredients

a. **Nutritional Powerhouses:** Include ingredients like quinoa, kale, spinach, spirulina, and hemp seeds. These nutrient-dense foods are rich in vitamins, minerals, and antioxidants, boosting the nutritional profile of your meals.

b. **Plant-Based Sweeteners:** Experiment with natural sweeteners like maple syrup, agave nectar, coconut sugar, or date syrup. These alternatives provide sweetness without the refined sugars found in traditional sweeteners.

c. **Asian Ingredients:** Explore the flavors of Asian cuisine by incorporating ingredients like miso paste, tamari or soy sauce, rice vinegar, nori (seaweed), and sesame oil. These ingredients can add depth and complexity to stir-fries, noodles, and dressings.

d. **Coconut Products:** Coconut milk, coconut oil, and shredded coconut can add a rich and tropical flavor to both sweet and savory dishes. Coconut milk is a versatile ingredient for curries, sauces, and desserts.

e. **Dried Mushrooms:** Dried mushrooms, such as porcini or shiitake, can add a robust umami flavor to your dishes. They can be rehydrated and used in stir-fries, soups, and risotto.

f. **Specialty Flours:** Experiment with flours like almond flour, coconut flour, chickpea flour, and buckwheat flour. These gluten-free alternatives can be used in baking, breading, and as thickeners in sauces and gravies.

g. **Aquafaba:** This is the liquid from canned chickpeas or the water left after cooking legumes. It can be whipped into a foam to replace egg whites in recipes or used as a binder in baking.

h. **Seaweed:** Explore the world of seaweed by incorporating nori, kelp, or dulse into your cooking. Seaweed adds a unique umami flavor and provides essential minerals.

i. **Plant-Based Yogurt and Milk Alternatives:** Experiment with plant-based yogurts made from soy, almond, or coconut milk. They can be used in baking, smoothies or enjoyed on their own.

Stocking your pantry with essential vegan ingredients opens up a world of creative cooking possibilities. You can create delicious and nutritious vegan meals by incorporating plant-based alternatives to animal products, essential pantry staples, and unique ingredients. Remember to explore different flavors, experiment with new recipes, and have fun as you discover the endless possibilities of vegan cooking.

CHAPTER 4

Cooking Techniques and Tips

Cooking is a creative and fulfilling activity, and mastering the art of vegan cooking opens up a world of delicious possibilities. This article will explore various cooking techniques and their benefits and provide kitchen hacks and time-saving tips for busy individuals. Whether you are new to vegan cooking or a seasoned pro, these techniques and tips will help you enhance your skills and create exceptional plant-based meals.

Sautéing and Stir-Frying: Sautéing and stir-frying involve cooking ingredients quickly over high heat with a small amount of oil. This technique allows vegetables to retain their texture, color, and flavor while developing a nice char.

Roasting and Baking: Roasting and baking are ideal for creating depth of flavor and achieving a crispy texture.

This technique is well-suited for root vegetables, tofu, and even fruits.

Steaming: Steaming is a gentle and healthy cooking method that helps retain the nutrients and natural flavors of vegetables. It requires minimal oil and helps vegetables maintain their vibrant colors.

Blanching: Blanching is a cooking technique that involves briefly immersing food items in boiling water or steam and then rapidly cooling them in ice water or under cold running water. It's a great way of cooking certain vegetables without over cooking them.

Grilling: Grilling adds a smoky and charred flavor to vegetables, imparting a unique taste to your dishes.

Blending and Pureeing: Blending and pureeing are techniques commonly used in making smoothies, soups, sauces, and dips. They create creamy textures and allow flavors to meld together. I recommend investing in a high-powered blender.

Kitchen Hacks and Time-Saving Tips:

a. **Meal Planning:** Plan your meals in advance to save time and ensure a well-balanced diet. Create a shopping list and prep ingredients ahead of time.

b. **Batch Cooking:** Prepare larger quantities of dishes and store leftovers for future meals. This saves time and effort while ensuring you always have a healthy meal on hand.

c. **Knife Skills:** Improve your knife skills to enhance efficiency in the kitchen. Learn proper cutting techniques to speed up ingredient preparation.

d. **One-Pot and Sheet Pan Meals:** Opt for one-pot or sheet pan meals that simplify cooking and minimize cleanup. Combine vegetables, grains, and proteins in a single dish for a complete meal.

e. **Pre-Cut and Frozen Ingredients:** Utilize pre-cut and frozen vegetables, fruits, and grains when time is limited. They retain their nutritional value and save prep time.

f. **Quick Pickling:** Preserve and enhance the flavor of vegetables by quick pickling. Use vinegar, water, salt, and spices to create a tangy accompaniment to your dishes.

g. **Spice Blends and Sauces:** Prepare homemade spice blends and sauces in advance to add depth and flavor to your meals. Store them in sealed containers for easy access.

h. **Slow Cooker and Instant Pot:** Utilize these time-saving appliances for effortless meal preparation. They allow you to set and forget, saving valuable time.

i. **Repurposing Leftovers:** Get creative with leftovers by transforming them into new dishes. Use roasted vegetables in salads or blend soups into sauces.

j. **Clean as You Go:** Keep your kitchen tidy and organized by cleaning as you cook. Wash utensils, cutting boards, and pans as you finish using them to minimize post-cooking cleanup.

Mastering the art of vegan cooking involves understanding different cooking techniques, exploring their benefits, and utilizing time-saving tips. By incorporating these techniques and tips into your culinary repertoire, you can create flavorful and nutritious plant-based meals while optimizing efficiency in the kitchen. Embrace experimentation, practice, and have fun as you elevate your vegan cooking skills to new heights.

CHAPTER 5

Creative and Nutritious Vegan Recipes

Following a vegan lifestyle does not mean sacrificing flavor or nutrition; in fact, it opens up a world of creative possibilities in the kitchen. In this chapter, we will explore a variety of vegan recipes that are both delicious and nutritious. From energizing breakfasts to vibrant salads, hearty mains, and guilt-free desserts, these recipes will highlight the versatility and abundance of plant-based ingredients, ensuring that you can enjoy a well-rounded and satisfying vegan diet.

Energizing Breakfasts

a. **Overnight Chia Pudding:** Combine chia seeds, plant-based milk, and your favorite sweetener. Let it sit overnight for a creamy and nutritious break-fast. Top with fresh fruits, nuts, or granola.

b. **Savory Tofu Scramble:** Crumble tofu and sauté with vegetables, turmeric, nutritional yeast, and spices for a protein-packed alternative to scrambled eggs. Serve with whole-grain toast or wrap it in a tortilla.

c. **Quinoa Breakfast Bowl:** Cook quinoa and mix it with plant-based milk, cinnamon, and a touch of maple syrup. Top with berries, nuts, and seeds for a satisfying and fiber-rich breakfast.

d. **Vegan Pancakes:** Prepare fluffy pancakes using a combination of flour, plant-based milk, and a bind-ing agent like applesauce or mashed bananas. Serve with fruit compote or maple syrup.

e. **Green Smoothie:** Blend spinach or kale with frozen fruits, plant-based milk, and a scoop of nut butter for a nutrient-dense and refreshing smoothie.

Vibrant Salads

a. **Rainbow Quinoa Salad:** Combine cooked quinoa with an array of colorful vegetables like bell peppers, carrots, cucumbers, and cherry tomatoes. Add fresh herbs, lemon juice, and a drizzle of olive oil for a refreshing salad.

b. **Roasted Beet and Citrus Salad:** Roast beets until tender, then toss them with citrus segments, arugula, and toasted walnuts. Dress with a simple vinaigrette for a vibrant and nutrient-packed salad.

c. **Thai Mango Salad:** Combine fresh mango, shredded cabbage, carrots, mint, and cilantro. Toss with a tangy dressing made from lime juice, soy sauce, sesame oil, and a touch of maple syrup.

d. **Mediterranean Quinoa Salad:** Mix cooked quinoa with chopped cucumbers, tomatoes, olives, red onion, and fresh herbs like parsley and mint. Drizzle with lemon juice and extra virgin olive oil.

e. **Grilled Vegetable Salad:** Grill an assortment of vegetables like zucchini, eggplant, bell peppers, and asparagus. Toss them with mixed greens, cherry to-matoes, and a balsamic vinaigrette for a hearty and flavorful salad.

Hearty Plant-Based Mains

a. **Lentil Bolognese:** Cook lentils with onions, garlic, tomatoes, and herbs to create a rich and savory sauce. Serve over whole wheat pasta or spiralized vegetables.

b. **Sweet Potato and Black Bean Enchiladas:** Stuff tortillas with roasted sweet potatoes, black beans, corn, and spices. Top with enchilada sauce and bake until bubbly and golden.

c. **Vegan Buddha Bowl:** Assemble a nourishing bowl with a combination of cooked grains, roasted or steamed vegetables, protein-rich legumes, and a flavorful sauce or dressing.

d. **Stuffed Bell Peppers:** Fill bell peppers with a mixture of cooked quinoa, black beans, corn, tomatoes, and spices. Bake until the peppers are tender, and the filling is heated through.

e. **Eggplant Parmesan:** Bread and bake slices of eggplant until crispy. Layer them with marinara sauce, vegan cheese, and herbs. Bake until the cheese is melted and golden.

Indulgent Yet Guilt-Free Desserts

a. **Vegan Chocolate Avocado Mousse:** Blend ripe avocados, cocoa powder, plant-based milk, and sweetener until smooth and creamy. Serve chilled with fresh berries or a sprinkle of cocoa nibs.

b. **Coconut Chia Pudding with Mango:** Combine coconut milk, chia seeds, and sweetener. Let it sit until it thickens. Top with fresh mango chunks and toasted coconut flakes for a tropical treat.

c. **Vegan Banana Nice Cream:** Blend frozen bananas with plant-based milk until smooth and creamy. Customize with add-ins like cocoa powder, nut butter, or berries for a guilt-free frozen dessert.

d. **Baked Apples with Cinnamon:** Core apples and fill them with a mixture of oats, cinnamon, nuts, and sweetener. Bake until tender and serve warm with a drizzle of maple syrup.

e. **Vegan Berry Crumble:** Toss fresh or frozen berries with a touch of sweetener. Top with oats, flour, coconut oil, and spices. Bake until the fruit is bubbly and the topping is golden.

These creative and nutritious vegan recipes highlight the diverse range of flavors and textures that can be achieved with plant-based ingredients. From energizing breakfasts to vibrant salads, hearty mains, and indulgent yet guilt-free desserts, there are endless possibilities to satisfy your taste buds while nourishing your body. Embrace experimentation, adapt recipes to your preferences, and enjoy the abundance of vegan cooking.

CHAPTER 6:

Veganism Beyond the Plate

Veganism extends beyond dietary choices and encompasses a lifestyle that seeks to minimize harm to animals and the environment. In this article, we will explore the ethical and environmental aspects of vegan living, as well as ways to incorporate cruelty-free choices in various areas of life. Additionally, we will provide tips for navigating social situations, dining out, and traveling as a vegan, ensuring that you can maintain your values and enjoy a fulfilling vegan lifestyle beyond the plate.

Ethical and Environmental Considerations

a. **Animal Welfare:** Veganism is rooted in compassion for animals. By adopting a vegan lifestyle, individuals refrain from supporting industries that exploit and harm animals for various purposes, such as food, clothing, entertainment, and testing.

b. **Environmental Impact:** Animal agriculture significantly contributes to greenhouse gas emissions, deforestation, water pollution, and habitat destruction. By choosing a vegan lifestyle, individuals can reduce their ecological footprint and contribute to a more sustainable future.

Cruelty-Free Choices in Other Areas of Life

a. **Clothing and Accessories:** Opt for cruelty-free vegan alternatives to leather, fur, silk, and wool. Choose garments made from synthetic materials, organic cotton, hemp, or sustainable plant-based fibers.

b. **Beauty and Personal Care Products:** Look for cosmetics, skincare, and personal care items that are not tested on animals and do not contain animal-derived ingredients. Choose brands that are certified cruelty-free and vegan.

c. **Household Products:** Use cruelty-free and environmentally friendly cleaning products, laundry detergents, and household items. Look for labels or certifications indicating that the products are not tested on animals and are made from sustainable ingredients.

d. **Entertainment:** Seek out cruelty-free forms of entertainment, such as attending animal-free circuses, visiting sanctuaries, supporting vegan-friendly festivals and events, and opting for cruelty-free alternatives to zoos and marine parks.

Tips for Dining Out

a. **Research and Plan Ahead:** Before dining out, research vegan-friendly restaurants in your area or at your travel destination. Use online resources, vegan apps, or community recommendations to find suitable options.

b. **Communicate Your Needs:** Inform the restaurant staff about your dietary preferences and restrictions.

Politely ask for vegan options or modifications to existing dishes, and most restaurants are willing to accommodate dietary requests.

c. **Be Adventurous and Flexible:** Embrace the opportunity to try new cuisines and flavors. Look for plant-based options or ask for ingredient substitutions. Asian, Middle Eastern, and Indian restaurants often have vegan-friendly choices.

d. **Check Ingredient Lists:** Be mindful of hidden animal ingredients in dressings, sauces, and condiments. Ask for ingredients or allergen lists if needed.

e. **Support Veg-Friendly Establishments:** Patronize vegan or vegetarian restaurants and establishments prioritizing plant-based options. Show your support and encourage others to consider plant-based choices.

Traveling as a Vegan

a. **Research Local Cuisine:** Familiarize yourself with the local vegan dishes or ingredients of your travel destination. Learn about traditional plant-based options and specialty vegan restaurants.

b. **Pack Snacks and Essentials:** Carry vegan snacks, energy bars, and travel-sized condiments. This ensures you have options if vegan food is scarce or limited during your travels.

c. **Communicate with Accommodation Providers:** Inform hotels or accommodations about your dietary preferences and inquire about vegan options for breakfast or other meals provided.

d. **Explore Local Markets and Grocery Stores:** Visit local markets and grocery stores to stock up on fresh fruits, vegetables, nuts, and other vegan ingredients. This allows you to prepare your own meals or snacks when dining out options are limited.

e. **Connect with Local Vegan Communities:** Utilize online vegan communities, forums, or social media groups to connect with local vegans. They can provide recommendations, tips, and insights into vegan-friendly places and hidden gems.

Navigating Social Situations

a. **Educate and Communicate:** Share your vegan lifestyle with friends, family, and colleagues. Explain your reasons for choosing a vegan lifestyle and its positive impact on animals, the environment, and your health.

b. **Offer to Contribute:** When attending social gatherings or potlucks, offer to bring a vegan dish to share. This ensures you have something to eat and introduces others to delicious plant-based options.

c. **Be Prepared:** Eat before attending events where vegan options may be limited. Carry snacks or a small meal if no suitable food choices are available.

d. **Engage in Constructive Conversations:** When faced with skepticism or criticism, engage in open and respectful discussions. Share information, resources, and personal experiences to help others understand your perspective.

e. **Seek Support:** Connect with local vegan groups, attend vegan meetups, or engage with online vegan communities to find support, share experiences, and seek advice on navigating social situations.

Remember, Veganism extends beyond the plate, encompassing ethical and environmental considerations, cruelty-free choices, and strategies for navigating social situations, dining out, and traveling. By embracing a vegan lifestyle in various aspects of life, individuals can align their values with their actions and contribute to a more compassionate and sustainable world. Remember to stay informed, be proactive, and seek support from the vibrant vegan community as you embark on your journey beyond the plate.

CHAPTER 7

Fitness and Well-being on a Plant Based Diet.

Maintaining fitness and well-being is crucial for leading a balanced and fulfilling life. Contrary to common misconceptions, a plant-based diet can provide all the necessary nutrients for physical and mental thriving. In this chapter we will explore how to excel physically and mentally on a vegan diet through exercise, self-care, and mindfulness practices. We will also address concerns related to veganism and athletic performance, highlighting the benefits and strategies for optimal well-being on a plant-based lifestyle.

Thriving Physically and Mentally

a. **Balanced Nutrition:** A well-planned plant-based diet can provide all the essential nutrients, including carbohydrates, proteins, healthy fats, vitamins, and minerals. To ensure a diverse nutrient intake, focus on incorporating a variety of whole plant foods, such as fruits, vegetables, whole grains, legumes, nuts, and seeds.

b. **Hydration:** Proper hydration is essential for physical and mental well-being. Consume adequate water throughout the day and incorporate hydrating foods like water-rich fruits and vegetables.

c. **Regular Exercise:** Engaging in regular physical activity is crucial for maintaining overall fitness. Choose activities that you enjoy, such as cardio exercises, strength training, yoga, or sports, to improve cardiovascular health, build strength, enhance flexibility, and boost mood.

d. **Adequate Rest and Recovery:** Allow your body time to rest and recover from exercise. Aim for 7-9 hours of quality sleep each night and incorporate rest days into your workout routine. e. Stress Management: Practice stress-reducing techniques like meditation, deep breathing exercises, or mindfulness to promote mental well-being. Engage in activities that bring you joy and relaxation, such as spending time in nature, pursuing hobbies, or connecting with loved ones.

Addressing Athletic Performance

a. **Protein Requirements:** Vegan or Plant-based diets can meet protein needs through plant-based sources such as legumes, tofu, tempeh, seitan, quinoa, and whole grains. Incorporate various protein-rich foods to ensure an adequate intake of essential amino acids.

b. **Iron and B12 Supplementation:** Pay attention to iron and vitamin B12 levels, as these nutrients can be challenging to obtain solely through a vegan diet. Consider supplementing with a quality plant-based iron supplement and regularly monitoring your B12 levels.

c. **Omega-3 Fatty Acids:** Include plant-based sources of omega-3 fatty acids, such as chia seeds, flaxseeds, hemp seeds, and walnuts, or consider an algae-based omega-3 supplement to support cardiovascular health and reduce inflammation.

d. **Pre- and Post-Workout Nutrition:** Prioritize pre- and post-workout meals that provide a balance of carbohydrates for energy and recovery, proteins for muscle repair, and healthy fats for sustained energy. Experiment with whole foods such as fruits, whole grains, nuts, seeds, and plant-based protein sources.

e. **Consult with Professionals:** If you have specific athletic performance goals, consider consulting with a registered dietitian or sports nutritionist specializing in plant-based diets. They can provide personalized guidance tailored to your needs and goals.

Mindfulness Practices for Holistic Well-being

a. **Meditation:** Incorporate a regular meditation practice to cultivate mindfulness, reduce stress, and enhance mental clarity. Start with short sessions and gradually increase the duration. There are various meditation apps and guided recordings available to support your practice.

b. **Yoga and Stretching:** Engage in yoga or stretching routines to improve flexibility, balance, and body awareness. These practices promote physical well-being, reduce muscle tension, and enhance relaxation.

c. **Gratitude Journaling:** Cultivate gratitude by keeping a journal and writing down things you are grateful for each day. This practice fosters a positive mindset, reduces stress, and enhances overall well-being.

d. **Mindful Eating:** Practice mindful eating by savoring each bite and paying attention to flavors, textures, and sensations. Slow down, chew your food thoroughly, and appreciate the nourishment it provides. This practice can enhance digestion and promote a healthy relationship with food.

e. **Self-Care Rituals:** Engage in self-care activities that nurture your well-being, such as taking relaxing baths, practicing self-massage, engaging in hobbies, or spending time in nature. Prioritize self-care to recharge and replenish your energy.

In conclusion, achieving fitness and well-being on a vegan diet involves embracing physical and mental practices that support overall health. By focusing on balanced nutrition, regular exercise, stress management, and mindfulness practices, individuals can thrive physically and mentally. Addressing concerns about veganism and athletic performance with strategic nutrient planning and professional guidance ensures optimal well-being. Remember, veganism extends beyond diet and encompasses a holistic approach to living in alignment with your values while prioritizing your health and well-being.

CHAPTER 8:

Raising Vegan Children and Families

Raising vegan children and embracing a vegan lifestyle as a family is an opportunity to instill values of compassion, health, and sustainability from an early age. In this chapter, we will explore the practical aspects of raising vegan kids, ensuring their nutritional needs are met, and engaging them in sustainable living practices. By fostering a vegan lifestyle in the family, we can nurture healthy, compassionate individuals who contribute to a more sustainable world.

Nurturing a Vegan Lifestyle for All Ages

a. **Educate and Communicate:** Explain the reasons behind choosing a vegan lifestyle to your children in an age-appropriate manner. Teach them about compassion for animals, the environment, and the health benefits of a plant-based diet.

b. **Lead by Example:** Embrace a vegan lifestyle as a family and demonstrate the values you wish to instill. Show your children that veganism is a joyful and fulfilling way of life.

c. **Include Children in Decision-Making:** Involve children in meal planning, grocery shopping, and cooking. Allow them to choose their favorite plant-based recipes and participate in preparing meals.

d. **Create a Supportive Environment:** Surround your children with like-minded individuals, whether it is joining vegan community groups, attending vegan events, or connecting with other vegan families. This provides a sense of belonging and support.

e. **Emphasize Variety and Balance:** Encourage your children to try various plant-based foods to ensure they receive diverse nutrients. Teach them about the importance of balanced meals and include a variety of fruits, vegetables, whole grains, legumes, nuts, and seeds.

Meeting Nutritional Needs

a. **Balanced Macronutrients:** Ensure your child's diet includes an appropriate balance of carbohydrates, proteins, and fats. Offer a variety of plant-based protein sources such as legumes, tofu, tempeh, quinoa, and whole grains.

b. **Key Nutrients for Growth and Development:** Pay attention to nutrients critical for children's growth, such as calcium, iron, vitamin D, and omega-3 fatty acids. Include calcium-rich foods like fortified plant-based milks, leafy greens, and tofu. Iron-rich foods include beans, lentils, fortified cereals, and green leafy vegetables. Consider supplementation of vitamin D and omega-3 fatty acids, if needed, after consulting with a pediatrician.

c. **Fortified Foods and Supplements:** In some cases, supplements or fortified foods may be necessary to ensure adequate intake of certain nutrients, such as vitamin B12 and iodine. Consult with a pediatrician or registered dietitian to determine if supplementation is required based on your child's specific needs.

d. **Diverse and Colorful Meals:** Make mealtimes enjoyable and appealing by incorporating a variety of colorful fruits and vegetables. Engage your children in meal preparation and encourage them to choose their favorite fruits and vegetables.

e. **Regular Check-ups:** Schedule regular visits with a pediatrician or registered dietitian to monitor your child's growth, development, and nutritional status. They can provide guidance and address any concerns related to a vegan diet.

Engaging Children in Sustainable Living

a. **Teach Environmental Awareness:** Educate children about the environmental impact of animal agriculture, deforestation, and climate change. Please encourage them to make connections between their food choices and the planet.

b. **Reduce, Reuse, Recycle:** Teach children the importance of reducing waste, reusing items, and recycling. Involve them in sorting recyclables, composting, and finding creative ways to repurpose items.

c. **Gardening and Growing Food:** Engage children in gardening activities to foster a connection with nature and an appreciation for the food they eat. Let them plant and care for fruits, vegetables, or herbs, and involve them in harvesting and cooking meals using the produce they have grown.

d. **Animal Sanctuaries and Volunteering:** Visit animal sanctuaries or engage in volunteer activities related to animal welfare. Show children the importance of compassion and respect for all living beings.

e. **Storytelling and Media:** Share books, movies, and documentaries that promote compassion, sustainability, and vegan values. Encourage discussions and critical thinking about the topics raised.

Raising vegan children and embracing a vegan lifestyle as a family is an enriching and empowering journey. We can foster healthy, compassionate, and environmentally-conscious individuals by nurturing a vegan lifestyle, meeting nutritional needs, and engaging children in sustainable living practices. Remember to lead by example, provide a supportive environment, and prioritize education and communication. Embrace the joys of cooking together, exploring new plant-based recipes, and celebrating the positive impact your family is making on the world.

CHAPTER 9

Building a Sustainable Vegan Future

uilding a vegan world is vital as we strive for a more sustainable and compassionate future. This chapter will explore the principles of conscious consumerism, the importance of supporting local and fair-trade products, and the power of advocacy and activism. We can contribute to a more sustainable, ethical, and compassionate world by embracing these practices.

Conscious Consumerism

a. **Ethical Considerations:** Consider the ethical implications of your purchasing choices. Research the companies and brands you support to ensure they align with your values, such as cruelty-free practices, sustainable sourcing, and fair labor conditions.

b. **Minimalism and Mindful Consumption:** Embrace minimalism by focusing on quality rather than quantity. Prioritize purchasing items that are necessary, durable, and ethically produced. Practice mindful consumption by evaluating your needs, avoiding impulse purchases, and reducing waste.

c. **Reduce, Reuse, Recycle:** Incorporate the principles of the circular economy by minimizing waste. Opt for reusable alternatives, recycle properly, and support companies that promote recycling and waste reduction initiatives.

d. **Sustainable Fashion:** Consider the environmental and social impact of the fashion industry. Choose eco-friendly and cruelty-free clothing made from sustainable materials such as organic cotton, hemp, or recycled fabrics. Support companies that prioritize fair labor practices.

e. **DIY and Upcycling:** Explore do-it-yourself projects and upcycling to reduce consumption and give new life to old items. Repurpose materials and find creative ways to reuse and transform them.

Supporting Local and Fair-Trade Products

a. **Local Food and Farmers' Markets:** Support local farmers and food producers by purchasing locally sourced fruits, vegetables, grains, and other plant-based products. Visit farmers' markets to connect with local growers and learn about their sustainable practices.

b. **Organic and Regenerative Agriculture:** Choose organic products whenever possible to support sustainable farming practices that avoid synthetic pesticides and fertilizers. Additionally, support regenerative agriculture focusing on soil health, biodiversity, and carbon sequestration.

c. **Fair-Trade Certification:** Look for fair-trade-certified products, such as coffee, tea, chocolate, and spices. Fair trade ensures that farmers and workers are paid fair wages and operate under safe and humane working conditions.

d. **Sustainable Packaging:** Support companies prioritizing sustainable packaging, such as compostable or recyclable materials. Reduce your reliance on single-use plastics by choosing products with minimal packaging or opting for package-free alternatives.

e. **Community Support:** Engage in community-supported agriculture (CSA) programs, join food cooperatives, or participate in community gardens to support local and sustainable food systems.

Advocacy and Activism for Compassion

a. Education and Outreach: Share information about veganism, its benefits, and its impact on animals, the environment, and human health. Utilize social media, local events, or community workshops to raise awareness and promote compassion.

b. Legislative Advocacy: Get involved in advocating for animal rights and environmental protection by supporting and promoting legislation that aligns with your values. Write to your elected representatives, sign petitions, and support organizations working on these issues.

c. Corporate Engagement: Encourage companies to adopt more sustainable and ethical practices. Engage in campaigns urging them to reduce their environmental footprint, eliminate animal testing, and provide plant-based options.

d. Volunteering and Donations: Contribute your time and resources to organizations that promote veganism, animal welfare, and environmental conservation. Volunteer at animal sanctuaries, support rescue organizations or donate to causes that align with your values.

e. Collaboration and Networking: Connect with like-minded individuals, organizations, and activists to collaborate on initiatives, share resources, and amplify your impact. Join local or online communities to stay informed, exchange ideas, and support one another.

Building a sustainable vegan future requires conscious consumerism, support for local and fair-trade products, and advocacy for a more compassionate world. By making informed choices, supporting ethical and sustainable businesses, and actively engaging in advocacy and activism, we can contribute to positive change. Together, we can create a future where compassion, sustainability, and justice are at the forefront, leading to a better world for all beings.

Finally: Congratulations on embarking on a journey toward a healthy vegan lifestyle! With the information, tips, and recipes shared in "Planting Change," you have the tools to nourish your body, mind, and soul while positively impacting the planet and its inhabitants. Remember, the key to a thriving vegan lifestyle is to approach it with curiosity, compassion, and an open heart. Enjoy the adventure ahead and savor the delicious flavors of plant-based living!